We Are
Here to Stay

We Are
Here to Stay

Tawfiq Zayyad

edited and translated
by Aida Bamia

SMOKE STACK BOOKS

Smokestack Books
1 Lake Terrace,
Grewelthorpe, Ripon
HG4 3BU

info@smokestack-books.co.uk

www.smokestack-books.co.uk

Poems copyright
the estate of Tawfiq Zayyad,
2022

Translations and
introduction copyright
Aida Bamia 2022

Arabic text edited by Merna Azzeh

ISBN 9781739772260

Smokestack Books
is represented
by Inpress Ltd

Contents

Introduction	9
I Shake Your Hands	13
I Would Have Fallen in Love, But...	14
Behind Bars	15
Evening Chat in Prison	16
Bitter Sugar	17
The Bridge of Return	18
The Crucified	19
A Long Story	20
Of Wine and Flames	21
The Burning Years	22
The Eagle of Joy	23
Remembrance	24
A Letter Sent Through the Mandelbaum Gate	25
Oh Moon, I Am Scared	27
We Are Here to Stay	29
The Fourteenth of July	31
Jumping Over the Bridge	33
About Men and Trenches	35
Lumumba	36
I Am from This City	37
Plant Me	38
A Nation Crucified	39
Beloved Umm Durman	40
Egypt in 1951	42
The Convergence of Roads	43
Qasidah Tahliliyya	44
A Mother Mourns a Son	45
Forbidden Matters	46
The Visible and the Hidden	47
A Strong Love	49
Reflections on the Invasion	50
To a Brunette	52

Introduction

Printed words do not often acquire a life of their own, flying off the page, outside the covers of a book and into the streets. But during the popular upheavals of 2021, Palestinian demonstrators spontaneously began chanting and singing one of Tawfiq Zayyad's poems, 'Unadikum' (translated here as 'I Shake Your Hands').

Set to music by the Lebanese Ahmad Qa'bur, the poem was very popular in the early 1980s. Forty years later, a new generation of Palestinians facing the forces of the Occupation made this poem their own, calling on everyone to rise up in a spirit of solidarity, and imploring Palestinians living in the West Bank and Gaza and in the diaspora not to forget their brothers in Israel, who had suffered longest under Israeli colonialism.

The phenomenon is not unusual in Arabic poetry (compare the popularity of Mahmoud Darwish's verses describing his nostalgia for the smell of his mother's coffee and her freshly baked bread). What was surprising however was the sudden and unexpected use of verses by a poet who, despite the abundance and diversity of his writings, has been neglected even among Palestinians, since his death in 1994.

This book is an attempt to provide readers with an insight into the life and soul of an impetuous man, and one who defies easy classification – poet, activist, friend, husband, father and lover.

In order to render the poems into English I have generally chosen accuracy of meaning over poetic feeling, conscious that I have not always been able to convey the full impact of the poetry. Rarely did I give precedence to an image at the expense of the meaning. I hope that these translations have done justice to the words of a great poet and a patriot.

Zayyad wrote patriotic poems, prison poems and love poems, and poems in solidarity with workers in the Soviet Union. He wrote about the suffering of the Palestinian people as a result of the harsh repression exerted against them by Israel, negating their rights, their aspiration for freedom and a decent living in their homeland.

There is a strong sense of solidarity with other revolutionaries and oppressed people in these poems, a sense of the suffering and endurance shared by people living under occupation. He wrote poems about Patrice Lumumba, Nazim Hikmet, the struggles of the Arab world against imperialism, the exploitation of Egypt by the monarchy, and all the hypocrites everywhere who exploit the weak and the poor.

Poetry and literature in general offer the unique possibility of mending pain with words, words of joy and words of sadness, words that bring tears and words that anger.

Like other Palestinian poets of the Nakba, it is the simple emotion of his poetry that moves the reader, and makes its way across fences, through prison walls and police controls, despite censorship and chains. It is the poetry saved in people's memories.

Aida Bamia, 2022

I Shake Your Hands

I implore you,
I shake your hands,
I kiss the ground on which you tread,
And I say: I will redeem you.
I offer you my eyesight,
The warmth of my heart I give you.
The tragedy I endure is my share of your plight.
I appeal to you,
I shake your hands.
I did not disparage my homeland,
Neither did I yield.
I confronted my gaolers, alone, naked, and barefoot.
My hand was bleeding,
Yet, I did not give up.
I maintained the grass over my forefathers' tombs.
I implore you; I shake your hands!

I Would Have Fallen in Love, But...

I would have loved to turn things around in a second,
To eradicate tyranny,
And burn every usurper

***

To make the poorest of the poor
Eat off gold and diamond plates
To parade in silk and gold trousers,
To demolish his hut and raise him

***

I would have loved if I could,
To turn the world upside down in a second.
But things are stronger than desires and anger.
You are consumed by your loss of patience,
Did it lead you to your goal?
Resist my beloved people,
Be patient as you face tragedies.
Aim at the sun
With nerves of steel.
Your arms can achieve the most beautiful dreams
And the most amazing things.

Behind Bars

Toss chains over chains
A chain is weaker than my forearms.
My people's love
My cherished struggle and my resistance,
Are the source of the determination
That burns in my blood,
It is the fire that devours terrible concerns.
My poems pour
The cup of humiliation over your troops,
And rub their faces in the mud,
While I raise my head,
And fill their eyes with my spit.
My resentment of this slave's life.
You, disfigured, coward, freak.
The warning sounds of the engine is deafening.
Do not think that the iron chain link
Can crush the lions' ardour.

Evening Chat in Prison

I remember, I do,
The Damoon, its bitter nights and its barbed wires,
Justice hanging on the fence, and
The moon crucified
On the steel window.
I remember plantations of red freckles
On the face of the pesky gaoler.

I remember, I do,
When we chatted in the dark night,
In the dusty Damoon cell.
We would sigh as we listened to a love story,
We would threaten when we heard the story of a theft,
But we cheered when a rebellious people achieved freedom.

***

Oh, my people,
Oh, sticks of incense,
You are dearer to me than my own life.
We keep the promise.
We endure life in a prison cell,
The ties of injustice and the prison bars,
If we endure hunger and deprivations,
It is to undo the shackles of the crucified moon,
To give you back your usurped rights,
To recuperate the future from the darkness of greed,
Lest it be bought and sold!
Lest the boat remains without sails.

The *Damoon* is an Israeli prison.

Bitter Sugar

Answer me,
Palestine, I call your wound drenching with salt.
I call it, screaming: let me melt away in it, then pour me.
I am your son, the tragedy left me here,
My neck under a knife.
I live on the rustle of nostalgia,
In my olive groves.
I write bittersweet poems for the paupers,
I write for the destitute.
I dip my pen deep in my heart,
In my veins.
I eat the hard steel wall,
I drink the October wind,
And I bloody my usurper's face,
With poems sharp like knives.
If the wreckage breaks my back,
I would replace it with a case
Made from the rocks of Hitteen.

The Bridge of Return

Dear ones,
I would cover the bridge of your return
With my eye lashes.
I would embrace your wound
And I would gather the thorns on the road
With my eyelids
With my flesh,
I would build the bridge of your return,
On the two shores.

The Crucified

My dear ones,
I am waiting for you
With flowers and sweets
I am waiting
With all my love!
I, the earth, and the moon,
The water spring, the olives, and the flowers,
Our thirsty farms, our roads, and a vineyard!
A thousand green poems
That cause the stone to bloom.

I will wait for you
With flowers and sweets,
I will wait for you with all my love.
I will scrutinize the wind
Blowing from the East
Hoping that its protective wing
Brings us news.
Hoping that the river shouts one day,
'Breathe a sigh of relief,
Your absent relatives
Have ferried across the river.'

A Long Story

I have a feeling it is a long story,
A trip on the wings of a beautiful nightingale.
I gather the stars,
I shape them into a necklace for your delicate neck.
And in the evening,
When the lights of the sky are turned off
And the white pillow embraces your inexperienced head,
My necklace would sleep peacefully,
With the doves
Over your budding silky chest.
I feel it will be a long story,
A trip over the wings of a beautiful nightingale.
Do not ask me how I knew, do not complicate matters,
Your eyes tell the story, they dictate my words.

Of Wine and Flames

I wanted to see you today,
You who dominates my thinking
I wanted to see you.
I picked up a rose as red as a carnelian,
And I stood at the corner.
When you appeared like a bright morning,
I felt about to reveal my secret.
I kissed my rose,
I whispered a few words,
Then I threw it to you.
As I was about to bid you goodbye,
I looked into your eyes,
I sent them two golden doves.
I gathered a fortune of jujube and sugar cane,
Over your tiny mouth.
I unfurled a rug of wine and fire,
Over your tiny cheek.

The Burning Years

for Nazim Hikmet

No! those poems were not composed in vain
Nor was the fiery tune blowing like a tornedo.
Those ten years were not spent in vain,
They made the flowers bloom in Anatolia.
No... those strings did not play in vain,
The digger's shovel did not dig in vain,
This mighty pen was used,
Only to reveal your destiny
Oh! Turkey, land of the free.

The Eagle of Joy

From the bottom of my heart,
From my open wound,
I sing for the boat, the Black Sea and the corals.
Long live Nazm's Turkey
Down with the Turkey of Adnan.

Remembrance

I have in the North region
An undaunted love,
A pure lily,
Dreaming of an encounter
A warmth, fragrant wish.
Her face extols her innocence,
Her cheeks are a captivating red
Her head is filled with lovers' thoughts.
Her eyes reflect uncertain joy.
She is my inspiration, the queen of my imagination,
The inspiration of poetic thinking.
I remembered, overcome with longing,
Our encounter in the hills of Nazareth,
As I was moved by the inflow of love,
She guides me to an irresistible paradise.
I bow to her youth,
I squeeze the unsullied lips.
What a soft mouth,
That a passing breeze would injure
Oh, what a limb, as if spring
Has bloomed in a rich garden.
I long for that hour of love,
It was a fascinating elation,
Its boons will live in my blood,
Its incense will fill my memory.

A Letter Sent Through the Mandelbaum Gate

Beloved mother!
I send you two hundred kisses,
From our house on top of the hill,
From the Ruta tree, the rose tree, and the Indian jasmine,
From the joyful ground tickled by animal feed,
From the setting for the olives and the buttress,
From the fasting stove, the sticks, and the pot,
From a grapevine that fills the basket every summer
From a Damascene mulberry tree, white and ailing,
From a premonition wondering when the night would end.

***

Mother, you are the most beautiful in the whole wide world,
You are the eyeball I adore, oh my heart!
To me, yearning is like a rose kept alive with my love.
Mother ...
How are you doing?! The heart is far away.
How is the black tent, the friends?
Tell me, by God, have you withered away as we did, wishing
             to be close to you?
We send you greetings, green like the grass.
The longing bird offers them to the flock,
He asks the stars about you, hoping for an answer
Asking about the first step on the road!
Our news, you ask? There is plenty to say, they break my heart:
Abu Salah lost his eyesight from grief,
Fakhri's mother, passed away grieving over Fakhri
The brunettes of the village have gone grey waiting.
The spring dried up and stopped flowing.
Our land is slipping away under the cover of darkness.
All that is left mother, is boredom and rocks.
But we resist, throughout the years, like iron,
How couldn't we not,
When the pride of the eagle is in our blood.

***

Your son is not alone any more, an only child since his birth.
I married the neighbour's daughter, sometime ago.
She is my support in a life filled with hardships.
If you see her you would say, 'she is the mint of the village'.
My apologies for failing to invite you on my wedding day,
I did not invite you because the road is blocked.

***

Mother, you have become a grandmother,
I have now from your flesh and mine, a rose,
A naughty three-year-old, like a monkey.
I called her Fahda, she is so sweet.
She asks me every morning, 'Where is my grandmother?!'
She loves Fairuz;
Her favourite song is *The Return*.

Oh Moon, I Am Scared

I am scared oh moon!
Scared of the night, of you, of your shattered light
My older brother, left this morning and has not come back yet
My mother is standing at the door, worried, waiting.
She stares at the faces of the passers-by,
Asking this one and that one, with a heavy heart,
'Did you find him? Did you see him...? Oh my God!'
Desperate, she returns and collapses
On the doorstep, a storm of tears,
She comes to me, kisses me and says,
'...He might come.'
Then she drags me to the gloomy alley,
To stare at the faces of the passers-by.

***

He woke up in the morning, as usual,
Whistling a sad, sad tune,
Whistling about the sun, the land, and the refugees!
About a homeland that would not be lost,
About usurpers,
And about a hope that would revive the dead.
He came to me,
Looked me in the eye,
And at everything in our room, everything.
There was in his eyes, thousands of strange sparks
And a thousand affectionate feelings.
He picked up his trousers and a shirt with beautiful prints.
He gave me a handful of coins
Then bid me
Goodbye
Goodbye,
Goodbye
There were, in his eyes, a thousand unusual glows,
And a thousand affectionate feelings.

He met my little face
With his tears.
And left with a sad, sad tune, whistled between his lips.
A tune about the sun, the land and the refugees,
About the rights of a dispossessed people,
About exploiters,
About a hope that would revive the dead.
I wonder... if the morning farewell,
Was the last farewell...?

***

The land shakes under distant footsteps,
Heavy, heavy, heavy,
Is it the sound of iron footsteps on the road.
We spot in the light, a gang of soldiers
My mother shouts, and collapses, a bundle of worry.
The soldiers get close to our door,
I cry.
Speechless, my mother crawls, oblivious,
She collapses and me too,
Over a white sheet, coloured with blood stains,
'Take him, we killed him there, at the borders.'
A tear spurts over my mother's face, then another, and another...
We cry and cry and cry,
A despicable, icy doll, summons us,
'Without tears, without tears!'

We Are Here to Stay

We are like a multitude of impossibilities
In Lydda, Ramleh and Galilea.
Here we will stay, a weight on your heart,
Like a wall.
In your throats,
We are like a piece of glass, like a prickly pear.
And in your eyes,
We are a fire storm.
We are here to stay, like a wall over your chests.
We clean the dishes in bars
We fill the glasses of the masters,
We sweep the floors in the black kitchens,
To provide for our children,
Ripped from within your blue jaws
Here we will stay, over your chests, like a wall,
We endure hunger and thirst; we are defiant.
We recite poetry,
We fill the angry streets with demonstrations,
We fill the prisons with pride.
We make children, one revolted generation after another,
Like a multitude of impossibilities,
In Lydda, Ramleh and Galilea.
We are here to stay,
So, drink the sea.
We protect the shade of the fig and olive trees,
We implant ideas like yeast in the dough,
Our nerves are cold like ice
While hell's fire burns in our hearts.
We squeeze the rocks to quench our thirst,
We eat dirt when we are hungry, but we won't leave!
We generously give our precious blood, generously,
       generously!
Here we have a past, a present and a future.

***

We are like a multitude of impossibilities,
In Lydda, Ramleh and Galilea.
We hold fast to our roots,
Our origins are deep in the ground.
It would be better for the oppressor to revise his accounts,
Before the thread comes undone.
For every action the book
Provides our answer!

The Fourteenth of July

I hang this head
To remind those who forget,
I did hang it, and vengeance is alive
Like a wedding celebration in my blood!
I hang this wolf,
This vile adulterer.
I wove the rope
On the loom of grudge.
I wove the rope with his blood,
Things woven in blood do not wane.
Didn't he wave on his loom,
A rope with my blood?!
Hasn't he replaced our honour,
The glory of our Iraq with humiliation!
I hanged him today,
As he hung me before!
How often has this shoe
Stepped on my chest and on my head.
How often has this palm obstructed my breathing
As for this tooth
This yellowish molar, distorted like a plough,
Hasn't it breathed the poison of death
In my plate and my glass.
And this head,
And this harsh stone-like heart,
I hanged it
I want to relive my celebrations.

I am the giant of this earth,
I will accept no one to own it, other than me!
I am the giant of its Dejla
I am the god of its magical Tigris
This oil is mine,
The gold of the mines is my own.
I swore,
To return to the eagle its nest,
I hanged it,
I threw the crown in the tomb,
To save Iraq's cabin,
Let the blood of the palace be shed.

I hung this head,
For those who forget, so they can remember,
I hung it, and the revolutionary is alive
Celebrating a wedding in my blood.
I hung it today,
But he hung me yesterday.

Damon prison, 1958

Jumping over the Bridge

Listen to the passing breeze,
The world announcing daytime
His chest is heavy with the secret,
Giving his lips permission to reveal the secrets.
Listen carefully, to the whisperings and
A conversation occurring in every house.
The crisping sound of the doors, fissured with the passing of time,
Rising in the quiet of the magic.

Look around, Baghdad's horizon
Is filled with clouds,
Sprinkled with fire,
There is on every handle, a free hand,
Turning with energy and fury.
The inhabitants of Baghdad,
Call each other, like wild lions.

There appeared among the crowds,
A man unlike any other,
His burning determination fills his eyes,
As if a thousand intractable devils inhabit them.
'People of Iraq, the country's bloody chest,
They erected on it these fortresses
The swings are still fed with the workers and the farmers.
Struggle, struggle, our energetic people,
Its damned heat is seeping to our side;
We either win or face annihilation,
Over a lake filled with the blood of the unjust.'

The cheering became louder, saying,
'The people are more powerful...'
From the residences of the feudalists,
A giant rose from the smoke of the fight
At his feet came a revolution,
Burning like a piece of Hell!

***

Iraq has turned into a large prison,
The leaders have justified the blood like wine.

***

The people, however, did not fear what he was facing

***

Saleh left and al-Said will follow.
The people of Iraq are eternal.

***

Oh bridge, I am not mourning you,
We are a people that sacrifices itself, smiling
I am not crying for you, I am not holding funerals
Crying is forbidden in our moto.
Our wounds do the talking.

About Men and Trenches

A forest of dishevelled men and guns
The horizon swelling with songs and banners,
To you the greeting of arms!
To the blood, the dirt, the wounds,
To the blaze that brought peace,
Oh caves!
Algeria, today
The fires will be extinguished,
Celebrations will fill the angry eyes,
The red eyes armed
With a thousand spears and a thousand she camels

***

Algeria, seven years have passed
You did not take time to cry
You did not let a minute pass without struggle
Without starting fires on the ground,
During the morning fierce battle.
You saved all your tears for the day the roses would
Grow on the nozzle of the weapon

Freedom! Your blooded face was lit by a righteous cause
It cost us the lives of a million martyrs.
Let the festivities begin
On top of your proud top, Oracy.
Let the children rejoice,
In the generous shade of the hero's arms,
The struggle is not over.
Brothers, the struggle is not over.
The forest of the dishevelled men and the guns
Will not put down their weapons,
It will only change trenches!

Lumumba

If you intend to weep, my bereaved eye, tell me,
Or did your tears dry up, sometime ago, on the long road,
A road where the free people trod, the best of all generations.
How many martyrs are lying on it, how many fatalities!
Yet, it is the path of the heroes, those who tackle the impossible.

***

The eagle, died defending his noble aim
His blood was treated like the blood of a mean slave
He lived like the sun, spreading the wings of light on the plains.
The assault of pernicious evil did not bend his proud head
Band of oppressors, roam freely and spread misery
Only few minutes are left for darkness, for the intruding epidemic.
We will run the knife of deliverance over you, in length and width,
We will carry on until history gets its revenge.

***

Oh, hero who was boiled at the hands of criminals
Whose death put an end to the words of the liars.
Cry? I have no tears left, I choked with them years ago.
Feel sad? Tragedies have turned our sadness into deep hatred.
You honoured death, oh, if the oppressors and the defilers only knew

***

Oh brothers carrying guns and arrows around your waist,
In the heart of black Africa, in the green plants of the
    mountain trails,
Peace, you say peace? Peace is not having the oppressors step
    on people's necks
Step on the holy flames, like the free and feared,
Let the precious blood colour every inch of the land.

I Am from This City

I am from this city,
From its sad dead-end streets
From the veins of the scaffoldings of its poor people's houses
From the heart of the sturdy fetlocks

I am from the Earth Day Street,
From the May's Place,
From the Sabra and Shatila's open courtyards
From the alleys where the police do not dare enter,
When people's anger projects flames.

Plant Me

Plant me like a red lily in your chests,
On all entrances.
Hug me like a green meadow,
One that cries, prays and fights.
Use me as a boat made of rosewood,
And the leaves of thickets.

I am the voice of the town crier,
I am the guide of the caravans.
My blood is made of flowers and sun
And the waves of grain spikes
I am a volcano of growth and youth.
My cheers are torches.

Oh People! I give you my life,
My song,
And I will always fight.
Come then, with your hands,
Your picks,
Let's demolish injustice
To build a free and just future.
Children, oh green basil,
Oh flock of nightingales.
For you we saved the roots of figs, olives,
And the rocks.
For you we protected the houses.

Oh unhappy people
Oh struggling people,
Those flags will not fall,
So long as we sing and fight,
A country that dreams of bread and books,
Of an honest living and tranquillity.

A Nation Crucified

They hanged us, a whole nation, on the cross,
They want us to repent.

This is not the end of the world,
Neither are we slaves.

So, dry your tears
Bury the dead,
And stand up again.

Oh, sad people,
You are the world
You are the only source of good.

You are History,
And the smiling future,
In this world.

Come, let's hold hands,
And walk over the flames,
The future of the free, no matter how remote,
It will happen soon.

Beloved Umm Durman

Hand me a piece of sugar,
For two years, I felt a bitter taste in my throat.
Give me a piece of sugar,
Umm Durman is calling.
It is holding a fragrant sword,
While I feel like a master,
Reprimanding and giving orders.
My whole being grows larger under the sun.

It grows larger while I feel my whole being elated and getting young.
Hand me a piece of sugar,
For two years I felt a bitter taste in my throat.
The shame I endured
Has turned my veins into stone.

Hand me a piece of sugar,
I feel as free as a child, now
My being is filled with springs of happiness.
I feel like a man in power,
Giving orders and issuing reprimands
I own everything around me,
I own the horizon, the land and the sea,
I own every shining star, I do!
Give me a piece of sugar, friend!
For two years I felt a bitter taste in my throat

I hate the patience of the defeated helpless,
The tears flowing down my people's eyes.
I have been feeling a bitterness in my throat.
Give me a piece of sugar!
I am happy now.

The joy of the sun and the shouting of the soldiers,
Are like a nightingale singing for a new dawn.
It is the joy of someone in love.

Open all the windows,
Draw all the curtains,
Open all the doors for the glad tidings,
Let the sun that we seek,
Enter my prison.
Let the wind coming from Sudan,
Tell me about the determination in the body of a revolutionary
Leave me alone now, to sing.
Umm Durman is at the gate!
Leave us alone today,
I and the love that arrived, unexpectedly.

Peace be upon you, my beloved brunette!
From all the vagabond orphans
Go forward, Oh the prettiest among my flags, go forward!

Egypt in 1951

Oh Nile, your shore reveals activities
The rocks of its tributaries are on fire
The bravery of your people fills you with praise.
History writes its story,
A nation recovers its glory
The glory that other nations know.

***

Your children defend you with their souls,
They were weaned with the concept of your liberation
Life would become unbearable with their anger
Their smile sweetens death.
Danger strengthens their arms
Victory lights their hearts.

***

Oh Egypt, your people are moving forward,
Defying fire and leaping forward.

***

John Paul led them,
They ripped you of your wealth, mercilessly.
They enjoyed bleeding you to death,
The pockets of the colonizer are full,
His body is covered with grease.
The palaces of the Pacha are filled

***

The crown is covered with precious stones
They are displayed, the fruit of your hard work
Let their arms be severed
Let them be trampled under the feet.

The Convergence of Roads

I came from a city hanging on a cross
I carry its greetings made of burning letters,
I carried them from my beloved homeland,
From the fugitives in the mountains and the valleys,
From those whose backs are ripped
With the whips of slavery

***

From our mothers wrapped in black,
From the eyes of the children,
From a jasmine tree that climbed on our fence,
Teasing the light of the day,
Smiling for the sun and blooming.

I carried it from my beloved homeland,
Hidden in my burning wound.
I freed it like a happy butterfly
In your vast horizon,
Oh Moscow,
Where all roads meet.

Qasidah Tahliliyya

Our Beloved left Tal'aat al-'Ayyuq
They left, alas, without bidding anyone, farewell.
I passed by in the morning to greet the mulberry tree,
No one was here to invite me in!
All I found was a weeping bird!
My feet froze on the thorns, as I remembered my beloved.
I asked the house about their whereabouts, it did not know,
My tears left a mark on their walls like flags,
Oh caravan leaders, if you happen to meet them one day,
Tell them that I am still crying over them;
Tell them that the eye of the lover has not been able to close,
The days of happiness are over, I wish they had lasted.
Tell those who left 'Tal'at al'Ayyuq,
No hardship lasts forever.

A Mother Mourns a Son

Send a word to his cousins, let them bring their drums and flutes
Tell them that the vulture of vultures, is back from his conquests.
Distribute sweets and bags of candy to all, young and old,
Rejoice Haniyya, rejoice
My eyes I give as your dowery, young woman.
Tell his cousins to come, like flocks of eagles.
Tell them that when he arrived, his eyes were on fire, glowing with
                                                                anger
'Give me our saved money, mother, the matter is serious,
I sold the wedding bracelet and my last ring
Celebrate and be merry, oh Haniyya
Do not leave him without a gun
Maids of the neighbourhood, prepare the animals for slaughter and
                                                        and light the fire,
Soak the clothes and the silk handkerchiefs in perfume, in vengeance
For Sarhan, the prince, son of a prince, of a prince,
Is back from his conquests to rest in my comfortable lap.
Young women of our neighbourhood,
We have cause to celebrate, use the tambourines
Tell his cousins to bring the drums and the flutes,
Tell them that he returned, I sell my last dress
With joy, mother marry him with the most beautiful girl,
In Celebration, mother sell your clothes and buy him a gun.

Forbidden Matters

My land, its earth,
My stolen treasure... My History
My father's and my grandfather's bones
Are not accessible to me;
How can I forgive?
I won't forgive even if they prepare to hang me.
Our green villages
Are covered with our blood,
Solely, difficulties remained.

The Visible and the Hidden

Do not tell me,
Do not tell me,
I am coming
From the place where every mouth has a guardian
And the informant stands on the curtains,
Where the ten commandments
Reverse the decisions of the courts,
And the slogans.
Where the echo and the shadow
Deny their origins
Where he who pleases its Creator is a risk-taker!
Do not tell me, do not tell me,
I am coming.
From where the conscience catches fire
Where the sulphur whispers
In the veins of the revolutionary;
Where the streets are shifting,
With human processions
No one can see their end.
They move where the spaces are full of trees
Like flags of people
Who will not immigrate,
Where miseries make heroes
Where the complaint
Indicates every weak man,
Where the voices of the children, the workers and the poets
Fill our horizon
With good news.

***

Do not tell me, do not tell me
I whose canines have appeared
Would be deceived by appearances?!
Light and tragedy,
Said to me, 'damn you, dig
Deeper, below the appearances.'
Nothing remains the same
Time is a moving force
There is an end to the night
No matter how long it feels.

A Strong Love

I will die because of my love;
When I die, it won't be
Out of sadness or melancholy,
Rather from the strength of my love!

***

For you my occupied homeland,
For you the Jasmin flower
Grows proudly in the garden of the house.
For you drops of rain make their appearance,
Shining in the face of death!
Have you heard about the love that kills?!
This is, people, the love that kills

***

Because of my deep love,
One day I will die, if I am to die,
Not out of sadness or misery,
Rather from the depth of my love.

***

Have you heard of the love that kills,
This is,
People,
The love that kills.

Reflections on the Invasion

Yesterday we did not float on a handful of water
We won't, therefore, drown in a handful of water.
They passed from here moving East like a black cloud,
Killing flowers, children, wheat and the drops of dew,
Justifying aggressions, hatred, tombs and spaces,
From here they will return, no matter how long it takes.
He died on the sand, without grieving,
From a bullet to his head, he shouted, helpless but with threats.
The killer encrusted a new number on his cannon,
Then went on, like a wolf, looking for a new victim.
A few meters away, a newborn cried,
When an iron chain passed over his forehead.
Do not say, 'we are victorious!'
This victory is worse than a defeat.
We do not look at appearances,
We rather see the extent of the crime...
Do not tell me, 'We are victorious!'
We are familiar with this kind of bravery,
We know the magician who gives the signal!
He is your master, panting, in his last breath.
We pull him from his nose,
To the disgusting tomb.
What do you have hidden for tomorrow?!
You who shed my blood,
Took away my vision and crucified my pen,
You who robbed a peaceful people of his right.
What do you have in store for tomorrow?
You who offended my flag,
Who opened wounds in my wounds,
You stabbed my dream,
What do you have in store for tomorrow?
Tomorrow is not defeated!
For twenty years you have been reviving
The rhyme of a summer dream,

You fish, at the order of others,
In the sea of blood and tears.
You build for the present, while we erect buildings for tomorrow.
We are deeper than a sea,
We are higher than the sky lanterns.
We have breath,
Longer than this stretch
In the heart of space.
We wonder which mother bequeathed you
With half the canal?!
Who is the mother who endowed you with a side of the
River Jordan,
Sinai and that mountain?
Whoever robs the right of others by force,
How can he protect his right when the scale tilts?!
Then what? I do not know,
I only know that the world and the years are loaded,
I only know that what's right does not perish,
It does not fall victim to usurpers.
No conquerors have ever lasted on my land,
So, lift your hands off our people!
We do not rob antiquities

***

We do not exploit the weakness of others
We repeat it for a thousand times
No, by this given light
We will not lose a speck of this soil,
We will never bend an inch, to flames and steel.

To a Brunette

Don't you see, my brown-haired girl
What I am enduring?!
She lives in my heart, but does not feel it!
The sparrow asks me about my illness,
While my illness is due to your eyes, I do not deny it.
I could not sleep the whole night,
Yet I did not stay late before.
I came to hunt you, but I was hunted
By the night, the sapphire, and the amber.
Bitter is what you endure in the name of love,
I will do whatever you order.

***

The fortune tellers in my hometown are exhausted
Asking whether my night would be moonlit.
They pleaded with the stars and asked,
Then announced the joyful news

***

Oh sugar cane, our window
Overlooks a vast distance, if you see it.
I stand there every day,
Wondering to the road, when she passes by?

***

You with silky hair, a soft night,
Whose phantoms bewitch
It is enough for me if a hand reveals its secrets
Smelling her makes me drunk.
You with the mouth shaped like a date, I am here,
If you are not meant to be mine, for whom do you bear fruit!
Your extreme charm
Made me fast for a long time,
When can I break my fasting?

***

You hurt/bruised my eyes, what would I do,
You wounded me and I do not bleed?
If my ardent love reveals itself to me,
Oh handsome one, it is then asking for forgiveness!

إلى أسمر

ألا ترى مابي يا أسمر
تعيش في قلبي ولا تشعر
يسألنيتي عيناك .. لا أنكر
أسهرتني ليلي على طوله
وكنت من قبلك لا أسهر
أتيت أصطادك فاصطادني
الليل والياقوت والعنبر
مر الذى أصبيت باسم الهوى
فليس يأتي غير ما تأمر

***

أتعبت أهل السحر في بلدتي
أسأل عن ليلي هل يقمر
فابتهلوا للنجم واستفسروا
وبشروا ياطيب مابشروا

***

يا قصب السكر شبّاكنا
يرمي لدرب العين لو تنظر!
وكل يوم فيه وقفة
أسأل الدرب متى تعبر؟

***

ويا حرير الشعر يا ليلة
ناعمة أطيافها تسحر
حسبي يد تفتض أسرارها
أو شمة منها دمي يسكر
يابلح الثغر أنا هأ هنا
إن لم تكن لي فلمن تثمر
أنا على ما فيك من فتنة
صمت زماناً فمتى أفطر؟

***

يا جارح العينين ما حيلتي
البلبل عن علّتي ... وعلي ولا أقطر؟
إذا تعرى الصب في بوحه
فانه يا حلو يستغفر!

إننا أعمق من بحرٍ، وأعلى
من مصابيح السماء
إن فينا نفساً
أطول من هذا المدى الممتدّ
في قلب الفضاء

أيّ أم، أورثتكم – يا ترى
نصف القنال
أيّ أم، أورثتكم ضفة الأردن
سيناء.. وهاتيك الجبال
إن من يسلب حقاً بالقتال
كيف يحمي حقه يوماً
إذا الميزان مال؟؟

ثم.. ماذا بعد، لا أدري ولكن
كل ما أدريه أن الأرض حبلى
والسنون
كل ما أدريه أن الحقّ لا يفنى
ولا يقوى عليه غاصبون
وعلى أرضي هذي
لم يعمّر فاتحون

فارفعوا أيديكم عن شعبنا
نحن لا نسرق آثاراً قديمة
ولا نبتز ضعف الآخرين
إننا للمرة الألف نقول:
لا وحقّ الضوء..
من هذا التراب الحُرّ
لن نفقد ذرّة..

إننا لن ننحني للنار والفولاذ يوماً.. قيد شعره

إن هذا النصر شرّ من هزيمة
نحن لا ننظر للسطح، ولكنا
نرى عمق الجريمة
لا تقولوا لي: انتصرنا..
إننا نعرفها هذي الشطارة
إننا نعرفه الحاوي الذي
يعطي الإشارة
إنه سيّدكم – يلهث
في النزع الأخير
إننا نسحبه – من أنفه – سحباً
إلى القبر الحقير

ما الذي خبأتموه لغدٍ
يا من سفكتم لي دمي
وأخذتم ضوء عيني
وصلبتم قلمي
واغتصبتم حقَّ شعبٍ آمنٍ
لم يُجرمِ
ما الذي خبأتموه لغدٍ
يا من أهنتم علمي
وفتحتم في جراحاتي جراحا
وطعنتم حُلمي
ما الذي خبأتموه لغدٍ
إن غداً لم يهزمِ

إنكم تحيون من عشرين عاماً
حلم صيفٍ ذا رواء
وتصيدون لأمر الغير
في بحر دموعٍ، ودماء
إنكم تبنون لليوم، وإنا
لغدٍ نعلي البناء

كلمات عن العدوان

يا بلادي..
أمس لم نطفُ،
على حفنة ماء
ولذا
لن نغرق الساعة،
في حفنة ماء

من هنا مرّوا إلى الشرقِ
غماماً أسودا
يطأون الزهر، والأطفال، والقمح،
وحبات الندّى
ويبيضون عداوات، وحقدا،
وقبورا، ومدى
من هنا سوف يعودون،
وإن طال المدى

هكذا مات بلا نعي..
على الرمل شهيد..
طلقة في رأسه..
صيحة قهر ووعيد
حفر القاتل في مدفعه،
رقما جديد
ومضى يبحث – مثل الذئب –
عن رقم جديد
وعلى بضعة أمتار بكى
طفل وليد
عندما مرَّ على جبهته السمراء،
جنزير حديد..
لا تقولوا لي: انتصرنا..

شدّة الحبّ

من شدة حبيّ سأموت
إن يوماً سأموت
لا حزناً أو حسرة
لكن.. من شدّة حبّي

لك يا وطني المحتل
لك يا زهرة فُلّ
تترقرق في صمت
تتلألأ في وجه الموت
أسمعتم بالحب القاتل؟؟
هذا هو.. يا شعب
الحب القاتل..

من شدة حبيّ سأموت
إن يوماً سأموت
لا حزناً أو حسرة
لكن.. من شدّة حبّي

من شدة حبّي
لك يا ومضة عزم
في عين مقاتل
لك يا ضحكة طفلٍ
يا ساعد عامل

أسمعتم بالحب القاتل؟؟
هذا هو.. يا شعب
الحب القاتل..

لا تحكِ لي.. لا تحكِ لي!
أأنا الذي نبّتُ
تخدعني المظاهر؟؟
الضوء والمأساة
قالا لي: لعنتَ، انفذ
إلى عمق الظواهر
لا شيء يبقى نفسه
والدهر
دولاب ودائر
ولكل ليل آخرُ
مهما بدا..
من دون آخر..

الظاهرة والعمق

لا تحكِ لي! لا تحكِ لي
أنا قادم
من حيث كل فم،
عليه حارس
والمخبرون على الستائر

***
حيث الصدّى والظلّ
ينكر أصله
ويسوط خالقه مغامر

لا تحكِ لي.. لا تحكِ لي
أنا قادم
من حيث تلتهب الضمائر حيث المآسي تصنع الأبطال
والشكوى
علامة كل خائر
حيث الشوارع زاحفات بالرجالِ
مواكباً
من دون آخر
حيث البحيرات التي
أمواجها أعلام شعبٍ
لن يهاجر
وحناجر الأطفال
والعمال
والشعراء
تملأ
أفق عالمنا
بشائر

محرّمات

أرضي .....!   ترابي ...!
كنزي المنهوب .... ! تاريخي
عظام أبي وجدّي
حرمت عليّ ، فكيف أغفر ؟؟
لو أقاموا لي المشانق
لست غافر
هذي قرانا الخضر
أضحت كلها دمناً
وأثاراً عواثر

أمّه ترثيه

شيعوا لبني عمومته ... يجيئوا بالطبول وبالزمور
خبّروهم أنه قد عاد من غزواته صقر الصقور
وزعوا الحلوى وأكياس الملبس للكبير وللصغير
بالهنا كل الهنا   ياهنيّة
وانكوت عيني أنا   ياصبيّة
شيعوا لبني عمومته ... يجيئوا مثل أسراب النسور
خبّروهم أنّه لما أتاني عينه جمر وشرّ مستطير
" ناوليني قرشنا الأبيض يا أمّاه فالأمر خطير "
بعت أسورة الزفاف وبعت خاتمي الأخير
بالهنا كلّ الهنا   ياهنيّة
لا تخلّوه بلا   بندقية
يا صبايا الحيّ هيئن الذبائح والمواقد والقدور
والثياب انقعنها بالعطر نقعا، والمناديل الحرير
إن سرحان الأمير ... بن الأمير ... بن الأمير
عاد من غاراته يرتاح في حضني الوثير
ياصبايا حيّنا   ياحراير
جاءنا الكيف فخذن ... المزاهر
شيعوا لبني عمومته يجيئوا بالطبول وبالزمور
خبروهم أنه إن جاء ثانيه أبع ثوبي الأخير
بالهنا يا أمه زفي إلى أحضانه أحلى صبيّة
بالهنا يا أمه بيعي ثيابك واشتري له بندقية

****

قصيدة تهليلة

أحبابنا شيلوا من "طلعة العيوق"
راحوا وما ودّعوا ياحسرتي مخلوق
مررت صبحا أحيي شجرة التوت
فلم أجد من يقول اليوم لي: تفضلي
ولم أجد ثم إلا طائراً يبكي
فجمّد الوجد أقدامي على الشوك
سألت داراتهم عنهم فلم تعلم
يادمع عيني على حيطانهم علم
ياحادي العيش لو يوماً تلاقيهم
خبرهم أنّي مازلت أبكيهم
وقل لهم أن عين العشق ما نامت
راحت ليالي الهنا .. ياليتها دامت
قولوا لمن شيلوا من "طلعة العيّوق "
ما شدّة عمرها دامت على مخلوق

****

ملتقى الدروب

أتيت في مدينة مشبوحة على صليب
معي تحية، حروفها لهيب
حملتها من وطني الحبيب
من المشردين في الجبال والسهول
من الذين شقّقت ظهورهم
سياط الاستعباد
***

من أمهاتنا الملفعات بالسواد
من مقل الأطفال
من ياسمينة تسلقت سياجنا
تعابث النهار
تضحك لشمس وتطلق النوّار

حملتها من وطني الحبيب
خبأتها في جرحي المشبوب
أطلقتها - فراشة سعيدة -
في أفقك الرحيب
يا موسكو
يا ملتقى الدروب

مصر ١٩٥١

يانيل وشطَّك يضطرمُ
وصخور روافده حممُ
وبطولة شعبك يهنؤها
أنَّ التاريخ لها قلمُ
وطن يسترجع ما عرفت
من عِزِّة ماضية الأممُ

يفديك بنوك بأنفسِهم
فعلى تحريرك قد فطموا
العيش يضيق إذا غضبوا
والموت يطيب إذا ابتسموا
والخطب يشدُّ سواعدهم
والنصر يضىء قلوبهمُ

يامصر ! وشعبك منطلق
يتحدَّى النار ويقتحم

ومضى "جون بول" يقودهمُ

نهبوا خيراتك مارحموا
وبعصر دمائك كم نعموا
جيب المستعمر متخمة
وبجسمه يلتفّ الدَّسم
والباشا أقصُره امتلأت

والتاج تزيّنه دررٌ
من كدح زنودك تنتظم
واليوم ... لتقطع أيديهم !!
وليسحق ... هامتهم ...قدم !!!

****

من عين شعبي.. يتحدّر

منذ عامين وفي حلقي مرارة
أعطني حبّة سكّر
فأنا الآن سعيدٌ

مرح الشمس وصيحات الجنود
بلبل ينشد للفجر الوليد
فرحتي
فرحة من أصبح..
في
حبّ..
جديد.

افتحوا كل النوافذ
وارفعوا كل الستائر
وافتحوا الأبواب، في وجه البشائر
ودعوا الشمس التي نحيا لها،
تدخل سجني
ودعوا الريح التي تأتي من السودان
تحكي لي، عن العزم الذي
في صلب ثائر
واتركوني وحدي الآن.. أغني
"أم درمان" على الباب.. اتركوني
اتركونا وحدنا هذا النهار
أنا والحُبّ الذي جاء على
غير انتظار
اتركونا.. وحدنا.. هذا النهار!

وسلاماً.. أنتِ يا فاتنتي السمرا
سلاماً!!
لكِ – من كل الصعاليك اليتامى
وأماما..
أنت يا زهرة راياتي..
أماما..!!

حبيبتي "أم درمان"

أعطني حبّة سكّر
منذ عامين وفي حلقي مرارة
أعطني حبّة سكّر
"أم درمان .." تناديني ...
وفي قبضتها، سيف معطّر
وأنا أشعر نفسي سيداً
ينهى ويأمر
رايتي تكبر في الشمس، وتكبر
وكياني كله –
يخضر نشوان ويخضر

أعطني حبّة سكّر
منذ عامين وفي حلقي مرارة
ومن العار الذي ذقت –
شراييني حجارة

أعطني حبّة سكّر
إنني – الساعة – كالطفل انطلاقاً
كل ما فيّ ينابيع سعادة
وأنا أشعر نفسي سيّداً
ينهى ويأمُر
كل ما حولي ملكي
ملكي الأفق
وملكي الأرض والبحر، وملكي ...
كل نجم ساطع .... ملكي وأكثر

أعطني حبّة سكّر
يا صديقي !! منذ عامين وفي
حلقي مرارة

***
وأنا أكره صبر العاجز المهزوم،
والدمع الذي

أمّة فوق الصليب

علقونا أمّة كاملة فوق الصليب
علقونا فوقه -
حتى ..
نتوب
هذه النكسة ليست
آخر الدنيا ...
ولا نحن عبيد

فامسحوا أدمعكم
وادفنوا القتلى
وقوموا من جديد

أيها الناس الحزانى
أنتم الدنيا
وأنتم منبع الخير الوحيد

أنتم التاريخ
والمستقبل الباسم
في هذا الوجود

فتعالوا
نشبك الأيدي بالأيدي
ونمشي في اللهيب
فغد الأحرار إن طال
وإن طال
قريب
****

بلد يحلم بالخبز
وبالكتب
وبالعيش الشريف
والسكينة.

****

إزرعوني

إزرعوني زنبقاً أحمر في الصدر
وفي كل المداخل
وأحضنوني مرجة خضراءَ
تبكي وتصلّي وتقاتل
وخذوني زورقاً من خشب الورد
وأوراق الخمائل
إنني صوت المنادي
وأنا حادي القوافل
ودمي الزهرةُ والشمسُ
وأمواج السنابل
وأنا بركان حبٍّ وصَبًا
وهتافاتي مشاعل
أيها الناس لكم روحي،
لكم أغنيتي
ولكم دوماً أقاتل
فتعالوا وتعالوا
بالأيادي،
والمعاول
نهدم الظلم
ونبني غدنا ..
حراً وعادل
أيها الأطفال ...
ياحبقاً أخضر
ياجوق عنادل
لكمُ صنّا جذور التين والزيتون
والصخر
لكمُ صنّا المنازل
أيها الناس الحزانى
أيها الشعب المناضل
هذه الأعلام لن تسقط
مادمنا ...
نغني
ونقاتل

أنا من هذي المدينة

أنا من هذي المدينة
من حواريها الحزينة
من شرايين بيوت الفقر
من قلب الثنيّات الحصينة

أنا من شارع "يوم الأرض"
من "دوّار أيّار"
ومن ساحات "صبرا" و "شاتيلا"
والزقاقات التي
لا تجرؤ الشرطة أن تدخلها
عندما يشتعل الناس غضبا ....!!

****

لومومبا

إن كان قصدك أن تسيلي ياعيني الثكلى .. فقولي
أم أن دمعك، جفّ في زمن، على الدرب الطويل
درب، مشى الأحرار فيه، صفوة من كل جيل
كم من شهيد فوقه متمدّد، كم من قتيل
لكنه... درب البطولة واقتحام المستحيل

....

النسر ! إنّ النسر مات، فداء مقصده النبيل
ظلت دماءه خسة العبد الأذل من الذليل
كالشمس عاش، يمد أجنحة الضياء على السهول
لم تحن هامته الأبيّة، سطوة الشر الوبيل

يا زمرة الطغيان صولي وانشري البلوى وجولي
لم تبق غير دقائق للظلم ... للوبا الدخيل
سنجرُ سكين الخلاص عليك، في عرضٍ وطول
ونجرّ ... حتى يصدر التاريخ مرويّ الغليل

-٢-
يا أيها البطل الذى غالته أيدي المجرمينا
ماذا أقول وقد عقلت بموتك الكاذبينا
الدمع ؟؟ لا دمع لديّ، فقد شرقت به سنينا
والحزن ؟؟ صيرت المآسي حزننا حقداً دفينا
بيّضت وجه الموت، لو يدري الطغاة والغونا

****

يا إخوتي المتزنّرين على البنادق، والحراب
في قلب أفريقية السوداء، في خضر الشعاب
يا إخوتي المتربصين، على الأعالي والهضاب
ملء المتاريس الخضيبة، والسراديب الغضاب
السلم؟ ليس السلمُ أن يطأ الطغاة على الرقاب
فامشوا على اللهب المقدس، مشية الحرّ المهاب
ودعوا الدم الغالي يلوّن، كل شبرٍ من تراب

لن تقذف السلاح
لكنها
تبدّل
الخنادق
....

عن الرجال والخنادق

ياغابة من الرجال الشعث والبنادق
يا أفقاً يموج بالنشيد، بالبيارق
تحية السلاح !!
للدم، للتراب، للجراح
لللهب الذي أتاك بالسلام
ياخنادق
اليوم ياجزائر
تنطفىء الحرائق
وتملأ الأفراح بالدموع الأعين الغضاب
الأعين المحمرّة التي تسلّحت
بألف حربة وألف ناب
****
سبع سنين
لم تذرفي الدموع ياجزائر
فلم يكن لديك لحظة واحدة
توهب للدموع
تضيع، تنقضي بلا كفاح
بدون أن يلتهب التراب في
ملحمة الصباح
وفرت كل مالديك من دموع
ليوم تنبت الورود فوق
شفرة السلاح

حق أضاء وجهك الأحمر ياحرّية
كلفنا مليون ثائر .. ضحيّة
فلتوقد الأعراس
في رأسك الأشم يا أوراس
ويمرح الأطفال
في ظلك الوريف ياسواعد الأبطال

لم ينته الكفاح
يا إخوتي .... لم ينته الكفاح
وغابة الرجال الشعث والبنادق

"صـالح " ولىّ، و"السعيد" سيمضي
إنما الشعب خالدٌ في العراق

****

ايه يا جسر ..لست أرثيك ... إنّا
أمة تبذل الضحايا وتبسم
لست أبكيك .. لست أنصب مأتم
إنّ في عرفنا البكاء محرّم
إننا، من جراحنا نتكلم

****

وثبة الجسر

أصغ السمع للنسيم الساري
يلثم الكون مؤذناً بالنهار
ضاق بالسرّ صدره فأباحت
شفتاه فضيحة الأسرار
أصغِ السمع !! .. ها هنا وشوشات
وحديث يدور في كل دار
وصرير الأبواب – شققها العتق –
تعالى في هدأة الأسحار
أدر الطرف .. أفق بغداد فيه
سحب حبلى وبلها من نار
وعلى كل مقبض كفّ حرّ
تلتوي في عزيمة واستعار
وعلى كل منحنى يتنادى
شعب بغداد كالأسود الضواري
....

وعلا بين ذي الجموع خطيبُ
رجل، ليس كالرجال، عجيب
ملء عينيه عزمه يتوقد
ألف شيطان فيهما يتمرّد:
"يارجال العراق، ياصدره الدامي ...
أقاموا عليه تلك الحصونا
الأراجيح لا تزال تغذّى
من جسوم العمال والزارعينا
تقحم سعيرها الملعونا
والفناء الفناء أو نجلب النصر
على نهرٍ من دم الظالمينا ..."
....
وتعالى الهتاف : "الشعب أكبر .. "
....
وعلا من معاقل الإقطاع
مارد شبّ من دخان الصراع
....

وذا البترول بترولي
وتبر مناجمي .. تبري
أنا أقسمت ..
أن أرجع وكر النسر للنسر
أنا علقتهُ ..
ألقيت بالتاج إلى القبر
فداءً لعراق الكوخ
فليسفك دم القصر ..

أنا علقت هذا الرأس
كي يذكر من ينسى
أنا علقته، والثأر يحيا
في دمي عرسا
أنا علقته اليوم ..
فقد علقني أمسا !!

سجن الدامون، ١٩٥٨

١٤ تمّوز

أنا علّقت هذا الرأسَ،
كي يذكر من ينسى
أنا علقته.. والثأر يحيا
في دمي عُرسا..

أنا علّقتُ هذا الذئبَ
هذا العاهر النّذلا
غزلت الحبل في صمت
على نول الضنّى غزلا
وغزل الدمّ لا يبلى
ألم يغزل على نوله
من دمي أنا حبلا؟
أما بدّل عزّتنا
ومجد عراقنا ذُلّا
أنا علقتُه الآن
فقد علقني.. قَبلا

وهذي النعلُ..
كم داست على صدري.. على رأسي
وهذي الكفُّ..
كم كانت تسدُّ عليّ أنفاسي
وهذا النّابُ..
هذا الأصفر المعوجّ كالفاس
ألم ينفث سموم الموتِ
في صحني وفي كاسي
وهذا الرأس..
هذا القلب المتحجرَ القاسي
أنا علقته حتى
أعيد اليوم أعراسي
أنا عملاق هذي الأرض
لن أرضى لها غيري
أنا جبّار دجلتها
وربّ فراتها السحري

كأننا عشرون مستحيل
في اللدّ، والرملة، والجليل ..
ياجذرنا الحيّ تشبث
واضربي في القاع يا أصول

أفضل أن يراجع المضطهد الحساب
من قبل أن ينفتل الدولاب
" لكل فعلٍ..." إقراؤا
ماجاء في الكتاب !!...
. . . .

هنا باقون

كأننا عشرون مستحيل
في اللدّ، والرملة ، والجليل
هنا .. على صدروكم، باقون كالجدار
وفي حلوقكم،
كقطعة الزجاج، كالصبّار
وفي عيونكم،
زوبعة من نار
هنا .. على صدروكم، باقون كالجدار
ننظف الصحون في الحانات
ونملأ الكؤوس للسادات
ونمسح البلاط في المطابخ السوداء
حتى نسلّ لقمة الصغار
من بين أنيابكم الزرقاء
هنا على صدروكم، باقون كالجدار
نجوع .. نعرى .. نتحدى ..
ننشد الأشعار
ونملأ الشوارع الغضاب بالمظاهرات
ونملأ السجون كبرياء
ونصنع الأطفال ... جيلاً ثائراً ... وراء جيل
كأننا عشرون مستحيل
في اللدّ، والرملة، والجليل ..
إنّا هنا باقون
فلتشربوا البحرا ...
نحرس ظل التين والزيتون
ونزرع الأفكار، كالخمير في العجين
برودة الجليد في أعصابنا
وفي قلوبنا جهنّم حمرا
إذا عطشنا نعصر الصخرا
ونأكل التراب إن جُعنا ... ولا نرحل !!..
وبالدم الذكي لا نبخل .. لا نبخل .. لا نبخل ..
هنا .. لنا ماضٍ .. وحاضر .. ومستقبل
. . . . . .

وخلف لي فوق وجهي الصغير
دموعاً تبلله ... فوق وجهي الصغير
وراح وفي شفتيه صفير حزين .. حزين
عن الشمس ، والأرض ، واللاجئين
وعن حق شعب سليب .. وعن غاصبين
وعن أمل يرجع الروح للميتين
تراه .. أكان وداع الصّباح
وداعاً أخير ..؟؟

. . . .

وترتجف الأرض .. وقع خطى من بعيد
ثقيل .. ثقيل .. ثقيل ..
على الدرب أحذية من حديد
ونلمح في الضوء شرذمة من جنود
وتصرخ أمي ... وتسقط كومة همّ
ويقترب الجند من بابنا
وأبكي أنا ..
وتزحف أمي خرساء ليست تعي
وتهوي وأهوي أنا
على شرشف أبيض
تلوّنه بقع من دماء
"خذوه .. قتلناه .. عند الحدود"
وتطفر دمعة
على وجه أمّي .. وأخرى.. وأخرى
ونبكي.. ونبكي.. ونبكي..
وتأمرنا دمية نذلة من جليد
"بدون بكاء ... بدون بكاء" !! ..

. . . .

خائفٌ ياقمر

أنا خائف ياقمر !! ..
من الليل ... منك ... ومن ضوئك المنكسر
"أخوي الكبير".. مضى لم يعد بعد ... منذ الصباح
وأمي في الباب موجعة – تنتظر
تحدّق في أوجه العابرين
تسائل هذا وذاك بقلب حزين:
" لقيته ..؟؟ شفته ..؟ ياللسماء !! .."
وترجع يائسة ترتمي
على عتبة البيت، عاصفة من بكاء
وتأتي إليّ تقبّلني :
" ... لعلّه يأتي .."
تتمتم في لوعة مرّة
وتسحبني للزقاق الحزين
نحدّق في أوجه العابرين

. . . .

أفاق كعادته - في الصباح
وفي شفتيه صفير حزين ... حزين
عن الشمس ... والأرض ... واللاجئين !!...
وعن وطنٍ لا يضيع .. وعن غاصبين
وعن أمل يرجع الروح للميتين ...
وجاء إليّ
وجال بعينيه فيّ
وفي كل شيء بغرفتنا ... كل شيء
وكان بعينيه ... ألف بريق غريب
وألف شعور حبيب.
تناول سرواله، وقميصاً بديع النقوش
وناولني حفنة من قروش
وودّعني ...
وودّعني ...
وودّعني ...
وكان بعينيه ألف بريق غريب
وألف شعور حبيب

. . . .

وابنك ما عاد كما خلفتَه وحدَه
لقد تزوجت ببنت الجار من مدّة
تعينني في عمري المملوء بالشدّة
إن تلمحيها ... قلتِ : ذي نعنعة البلدة
صفحاً ... أنا لم أدعكم في ليلة الصّمدة
لم أدعكم ... فالدرب يا أمي ... منسدّة

. . . .

وأنت قد أصبحتِ، يا والدتي، جدّة
لي الآن من لحمكِ .. من لحمي أنا وردة
شيطانةٌ ... في عامها الثالث كالقردة
أسميتها .. لله ما أطيبها ...فهدَة
تسألني كل صباح : " أينها الجدّة ؟! .."
تحب فيروز
خصوصاً : غنوة "العودة" ...

رسالة عبر بوابة مندلباوم

أمي الحبيبة !!
لكِ مني مئتا قبلة
أبعثها.. من بيتنا العالي على التلّة
من شجرة " الفيجن" والوردة والفلّة
والبيدر الضاحك من دغدغة الغلّة
من نصبة الزيتون والسدرة والملّة
والموقد الصائم... والعيدان ... والحلّة
من كرمةٍ... في كل صيفٍ تملأ السلّة
وتوتة شامية، بيضاء، معتلّة
وهاجس، يسألني.. عن آخر الليلة

. . . .

أمّاه ...
يا أجمل ما في العالم الرحبِ
ياحبّة العين التي أعبد .. ياقلبي
الشوق عندي وردة تحيا على حبي
أمّاه ...
كيف الحال ؟!. إنّ القلب يستنبي
وكيف حال الخيمة السوداء، والصحب ..؟؟
بالله هل ذبتم كما ذبنا .. إلى القرب ...؟؟
إليكم تحية خضراء ... كالعشب ..
الطائر المشتاق، يهديها إلى السّربِ
ويسأل النجمات عنكم علّها تنبي
متى تكون الخطوة الأولى .. على الدربِ ؟!..
أخبارُنا ...؟؟ كثيرة ..تثقل لي صدري :
أبو صلاح عميت عيناه من قهر
وأمُّ فخري .. ذهبت حزناً على فخري
والقرية السمراء .. قد شابت من الصبر
والعين شحّ الماء فيها، فهي لا تجري
وأرضنا ... يسلبها الظلاّم للغير
لم يبق يا أمي غير الملّ والصخر
لكننا ... نصمدُ ... كالفولاذِ ... للدهر
وكيف لا ..
وفي دمانا أنف النسر ....؟

ذكريات

ولي في ربوع الشمال غرام حييّ
وزنبقة طاهرة
تعيش على حُلمها باللقاءِ
على دفء أمنية عاطرة
على وجهها سمة الأبرياءِ
وفي خدّها حمرة آسرة
وفي رأسها فكر العاشقين
وفي عينها فرحة حائرة
هي الوحي لي وعروس الخيال
وملهمة الخطرة الشاعرة
تذكرت .. والشوق يغلبني ...
لقاءً لنا في ربى الناصرة
يهزّ كياني دبيب الهوى
وتأخذني جنّة قاهرة
فأعطف بين يديّ صباها
وأعتصر الشفة الناضرة
فيا له ثغراً تنعّم حتى
لتجرحه النسمة العابرة
وياله فرعاً .. كأن الربيع
تفتح في روضة عامرة
سويعة حبّ .. أحنّ إليها
فقد عشتها نشوة ساحرة
ستحيا أفاويقها في دمي
ويملؤ بخورها الذاكرة

. . . . . .

نسر الفرحة

***

من أعماقي .. من جرحي المفتوح
أغني للزورق.. للبحر الأسود... للمرجان
"تحيا تركيا ناظم
تسقط تركيا عدنان" !!..
. . . . . .

السنوات المحترقة

لا!! ... لم تذهب عبثاً تلك الأشعار
واللحن الثائر كالإعصار
لم تحرق تلك السنوات العشر
إلا لينوّر في الأناضول الزهر
لا ..
لم تعزف عبثاً تلك الأوتار
لم تهو سدىً فأس الحفّار
لم يتنفس ذاك القلم الجبّار
إلا ليخطّ مصيركِ ...
ياتركيا الأحرار...
. . . . . .

عن النبيذ واللّهب

أردتُ أن أراكِ
اليوم ياشاغلتي، أردتُ أن أراكِ
قطفتُ وردةً كأنها عقيق
ووقفت عند منحنى الطريق
وعندما طلعتِ كالصباح
أحسست أنني أهم أن أبوح
قبّلت وردتي
وشوشتها بكلمتين
رميتها إليك
وقبل أن أقول للقاء
نظرت في عينيك
أطلقت فيها حمامتين من ذهب
وفوق ثغرك الصغير
لملمت ثروةً من العنّاب والقصب
وفوق رأس خدّك النضير
سجّادةً من النبيذ واللّهب
. . . .

حكاية تطول

أحسّ أنّها حكاية تطول
ورحلة على جناح بلبل جميل
ألتقط النجوم ...
أشكّها قلادة، لعنقك الصغير
وفي المساء ...
وحينما تنطفىء السماء ...
وتحضن الوسادة البيضاء رأسك الغرير
تنام في سلام ..
قلادتي .. تنامُ في سلام
مع اليمام
في صدرك المفتح الحرير
أحسّ أنها حكاية تطول
ورحلة على جناح بلبل جميل
لاتسألي عرفتُ كيف، لا تعقّدي الأمور
عيناك تحكيان تمليان ما أقول.
. . . .

المصلوب

أحبائي ..
أنا بالورد والحلوى
وكلّ الحبّ أنتظرُ
أنا، والأرض، والقمر
وعين الماء، والزيتون، والزهر
وبيّاراتنا العطشى
وسكّتنا، وكرمُ دوال !..
وألف قصيدة خضراء
منها يورق الحجر

. . . .

أنا بالوردِ والحلوى
وكلّ الحبّ أنتظرُ
وأرقب هبّة الريح التي
تأتي من الشرق
لعلّ على جناح جناحها
يأتي لنا خبر
لعلّه ذات يوم يهتف النّهر:
" تنفس ... أهلك الغيّاب
يامصلوبُ ...
قد عبروا" !!..

. . . .

جسر العودة

أحبائي...
برمش العينِ
أفرش درب عودتكم،
برمش العين

وأحضن جرحكم،
وألمُ شوك الدَّربِ،
بالجفنين.

ومن لحمي ..
سأبني جسر عودتكم،
على الشطئين!!...
. . . . . .

السُكَّر المرّ

أجيبيني...
أنادي جرحك المملوء ملحاً، يافلسطيني
أناديه وأصرخُ:
ذوّبيني فيه... صبّيني
أنا ابنك: خلفتني ها هنا المأساةُ،
عنقاً تحت سكين..
أعيش على حفيف الشوق ...
في غابات زيتوني
وأكتب للصعاليك القصائد سكّراً مراً
وأكتب للمساكين
وأغمس ريشتي، في قلب قلبي
في شراييني
وآكل حائط الفولاذ
أشرب ريح تشرين
وأدمي وجه مغتصبي ...
بشعر كالسكاكين
وإن كسر الردى ظهري،
وضعت مكانه صوّانةً،
من صخر "حطّين" !!!
. . . . . .

سمر فى السجن

أتذكّر ... إنّي أتذكّر
"الدامون" .. لياليه المرّة، والأسلاك.
والعدل المشنوق على السور هناك.
والقمر المصلوب على..
فولاذ الشباك
ومزارعَ ... من نمشٍ أحمر
في وجه السجان الأنقر

. . . .

أتذكّر ... إني أتذكّر
لمّا كنا في أحشاء الظلمة نسمر
في الزنزانة ... في "الدامون" الأغبر
نتنهدُ لما نسمع قصة حب
نتوعد عند حكاية سلب
ونهلل عند تمرّد شعب ..
يتحرر

. . . .

ياشعبي ...
ياعود النّد ...
يا أغلى من روحي عندي
إنّا باقونَ على العهدِ
لم نرض عذاب الزنزانة
وقيود الظلم وقضبانه
ونقاسي الجوع وحرمانه
إلا لنفكّ وثاق القمر المصلوب
ونعيد إليك الحق المسلوب
ونطول الغد من ليل الأطماع
حتى لا تُشرى وتباع !!...
حتى..
لا يبقى الزورق ...دون شراع !!!...

مِن وراء القضبان

- ١ -
ألقوا القيود على القيود
فالقيد أوهى .. من زنودي
لي من هوى شعبي،
ومن حب الكفاح، ومن صمودي
عزم ... تسعَّر في دمي
ناراً على الخطب الشديد

يا طغمة أسقيتها..
كأس المذلّة، من قصيدي
مرَّغتها في الوحل حتى جيدها،
ونصبتُ جيدي
وبصقت ملء عيونها
حقدي على عيش العبيد

ياطغمة المسخ الجبان
يضج – موتور الوعيد
لا تحسبي زرد الحديد،
ينال من همم الأسود
....

أحبُّ.. ولكن

أحبُّ لو استطعتُ بلحظةٍ
أن أقلب الدنيا لكم رأساً على عقبِ
وأقطع دابر الطغيانِ
أحرق كل مغتصبِ
وأوقد تحت عالمنا القديمِ
جهنماً، مشبوبة اللّهبِ

وأجعل أفقرَ الفقراء يأكل في
صحون الماس، والذهبِ
ويمشي في سراويلِ
الحرير الحرّ، والقصبِ
وأهدم كوخه ... أبني له
قصراً على السُحُبِ

. . . .

أحبُّ لو استطعت بلحظةٍ
أن أقلب الدنيا لكم رأساً على عقبِ
ولكن .. للأمور طبيعةٌ
أقوى من الرغبات والغضبِ
نفاذ الصبر يأكلكم فهل
أدّى إلى إرَبِ؟؟
صموداً أيها الناس الذين أحبهم
صبراً على النوَبِ
ضعوا بين العيون الشمسَ
والفولاذ في العصَبِ
سواعدكم تحقق أجمل الأحلام ..
تصنع أعجَب العَجبِ

أشدُ على أيديكم

أناديكم
أشدُ على أياديكم..
أبوسُ الأرض تحت نعالكم
وأقول: أفديكم
وأهديكم ضيا عيني
ودفء القلب أعطيكم.
فمأساتي التي أحيا
نصيبي من مآسيكم.

أناديكم
أشد على أياديكم ...
أنا ما هنتُ في وطني
ولا صغرّتُ أكتافي
وقفتُ بوجه ظلاّمي
يتيماً، عارياً، حافي
حملتُ دمي على كفي
وما نكسّتُ أعلامي
وصنتُ العشبَ فوق قبور أسلافي
أناديكم... أشدُ على أياديكم !!
.....

قائمة المحتويات

أشدُّ على أيديكم	96
أحبّ.. ولكن	95
من وراء القضبان	94
سمر في السجن	93
السكّر المرّ	92
جسر العودة	91
المصلوب	90
حكاية تطول	89
عن النبيذ واللّهب	88
السنوات المحترقة	87
نسر الفرحة	86
ذكريات	85
رسالة عبر بوابة مندلباوم	84
خائفٌ ياقمر	82
هنا باقون	80
١٤ تمّوز	78
وثبة الجسر	76
عن الرجال والخنادق	74
لومومبا	72
أنا من هذي المدينة	71
إزرعوني	70
أمّة فوق الصليب	68
حبيبتي "أم درمان"	67
مصر ١٩٥١	65
ملتقى الدروب	64
قصيدة تهليلية	63
أمه ترثيه	62
مُحرّمات	61
الظاهرة والعمق	60
شدة الحبّ	58
كلمات عن العدوان	57
إلى أسمر	54

هنا باقون

توفيق زيّاد
ترجمة وتحرير
عايدة بامية